MW01169743

TRAVEL GAMES FOR ADULTS

BEX BAND

CONTENTS

1

INTRODUCTION

I'm very used to long travel days! Since going on my first big adventure in my late twenties, hiking 1000km the length of Israel, I've become addicted to going on adventures.

Whatever the adventure - kayaking the width of the UK, kick-scooting the length of the USA, or crossing the Jordan Desert - there's always a long travel day to get to the start and to get me home at the end.

On top of this, I also travel a lot for my job.

I've built a career for myself as an adventurer, sharing my explorations through talks and books.

I also founded Love Her Wild, one of the world's largest women's adventure communities (www.loveherwild.com).

Over the years, I've collected dozens of games, prompts and activities, designed to turn long and boring travel days into an opportunity for laughs, interesting conversations and memorable moments. I collected these from fellow travellers and also from the many summers I spent volunteering on summer camps with ATE Superweeks (www.superweeks. co.uk).

My collection turned into a small book, which I would always have on me for travel days for inspiration to keep myself and my passengers happy. After years of being asked about where I get my ideas from, I felt it was time to share my collection with the world. That's how this book came about!

2

TRAVEL GAMES

SIX DEGREES OF KEVIN BACON

NEED TO KNOW:

- **Number of players:** Minimum of 2 players, no maximum
- **Where to play:** Train, airplane, car

RULES:

- Someone names a random actor.
- Everyone works together to try figure out the shortest chain that links that actor to Kevin Bacon - the link can either be via movies or co-stars.
- Once you've tried a few rounds, you can pick a different well-known actor to replace Kevin Bacon, such as Morgan Freeman or Harrison Ford.

GRANNY'S LIKES

NEED TO KNOW:

- **Number of players:** Minimum of 2 players, no maximum
- **Where to play:** Train, airplane, car

RULES:

- The game leader starts by stating Granny's preferences, such as "My granny likes coffee but doesn't like tea" or "My granny likes buses but doesn't like trains."
- Other players then guess what Granny likes and dislikes. The leader confirms whether they are correct or not.
- The secret rule is that Granny dislikes words containing the letter 'T'.
- If someone works out the secret, they should keep it to themselves so the rest of the passengers can continue playing.

GEOGRAPHY GAME

NEED TO KNOW:

- **Number of players:** Minimum of 2 players, no maximum
- **Where to play:** Car, train, airplane

RULES:

- One player begins by naming a country, such as Brazil.
- The next player must name a country that starts with the last letter of the previously named country (e.g., Lithuania follows Brazil).
- If a player can't think of a country, they are out, and the turn passes to the next player. This continues until only one player is left, who is the winner.
- After playing with countries, you can change the theme to other categories such as animals, household objects, famous actors, films, or books.

SUITCASE, SUITCASE, SUITCASE

NEED TO KNOW:

- **Number of players:** Minimum of 3 players, no maximum
- **Where to play:** Car, train, airplane

RULES:

- Each player chooses an item they might find in their suitcase - like sunscreen, flipflop, or camera.
- The active player must repeat another player's chosen item three times in a row (e.g., 'camera, camera, camera') before the named player can respond by saying it once ('camera').
- If the active player succeeds before the named player responds, they become the new active player; if not, the initial player remains active and must try again.
- Items with more syllables are trickier to say quickly, so you might want to give an opportunity at some point for everyone to switch to a new item.

- The game is best played intermittently throughout the journey, catching other players off guard when they are distracted by reading or conversation. This is also a good game to continue once you've reached your destination.

GOING THROUGH CUSTOMS I HAD TO DECLARE

NEED TO KNOW:

- **Number of players:** minimum 2 players, no maximum
- **Where to play:** car/train/airplane

RULES:

- Start by saying, 'Going through customs, I had to declare...' followed by an item you might purchase abroad and the location you bought it from—the only stipulation is that it must rhyme. • For instance, "Going through customs, I had to declare jelly from Delhi" or "Going through customs, I had to declare a tunic from Munich." • See whose declaration garners the most laughter!

NAME THE ARTIST

NEED TO KNOW:

- **Number of players:** Minimum of 2 players, no maximum
- **Where to play:** Car

RULES:

- Have music playing on the car speakers - you can use the radio, but it's best to use a playlist with songs from different artists. (A 'road trip' playlist on Spotify would be perfect!)
- Each time a new song plays, the first person to shout out the name of the artist gets a point. Someone should keep a tally of the points on a piece of paper or on their phone.
- Once everyone is ready to move on to the next game, tally up the scores to see who the winner is.

HOT SEAT

NEED TO KNOW:

- **Number of players:** Minimum of 2 players, no maximum
- **Where to play:** Train, airplane, car

RULES:

- Player One begins by asking a question about themselves. It could be 'what was my first job?', 'what was my best subject at school?' or 'what was my childhood pet's name?'.
- The rest of the players take turns giving their answer before Player One says what the correct answer is.
- A correct answer means 1 point and a wrong answer means a point is deducted. Someone should keep track of scores as you go.
- Once Player One has asked five questions, move the 'hot seat' to the next player.

- You can play a second round, this time making the questions harder or more specific to make it more challenging.

QUICK-FIRE QUESTIONS

NEED TO KNOW:

- **Number of players:** Minimum of 2 players, no maximum
- **Where to play:** Car, train, airplane

RULES:

- Players take turns speaking.
- Players must continue the conversation by only asking questions. If someone hesitates or makes a statement, they are out.
- For example: "Are you ready to start?" "Why wouldn't I be ready?" "Do you think this will be fun?" "Why do you ask that?"
- The game continues until someone slips up, then a new round begins.
- This game is ridiculous but also surprisingly difficult and a lot of fun!

GHOST

NEED TO KNOW

Number of players: Minimum of 2 players, no maximum

Where to play: Car, train, airplane

RULES:

- Players take turns to say a letter, contributing to the formation of a word.
- Other players can challenge players at any time and request proof of the intended word.
- For instance, player 1 might say 'B' (intended word 'Ball'), player 2 'R' (Intended word 'Brain', and player 3 'E' (intended word 'Break').
- The player who says a letter that completes a word loses that round. For example, if the letters are 'B', 'R', 'E', 'A', 'T' and the next player has no option but to say 'H', they lose the round.
- When a player loses a round, they receive a letter from the word 'ghost'. The first player to collect all five letters, spelling out G-H-O-S-T, loses the game.

THE [INSERT] GAME

NEED TO KNOW:

- **Number of players:** Minimum of 2 players, no maximum
- **Where to play:** Train, airplane, car

RULES:

- Simply think of a well-known movie or book.
- Replace one of the words in the title with a different word - see which gets the biggest laugh.
- *'Gone With the ____', '____Wars', 'The Lion, the witch and the ____', 'When Harry Met____', etc.*

SILENT PICTURES

NEED TO KNOW:

- **Number of players:** Minimum of 2 players, no maximum
- **Where to play:** Train, airplane

RULES:

- Choose one player to be the mime artist. This player uses Google images or photos on a phone to select an image or painting.
- The other players each get a pen and paper.
- The mime artist has 5 minutes to silently act out the chosen image, using only gestures (no words or sounds). While they do this, the other players attempt to draw what they think the player is miming.
- At the end of the 5 minutes, everyone compares their drawings. The player whose drawing is the closest to the original image wins and becomes the next mime artist.

NAME THE MOST...

NEED TO KNOW:

- **Number of players:** Minimum of 2 players, no maximum
- **Where to play:** Train, airplane, car

RULES:

- Choose a category and take turns naming items related to that category. Examples include Disney princesses, famous rulers or Harry Potter characters.
- If a player takes longer than a few seconds to give an answer or repeats an answer already given, then they are out.
- Players continue until there is one player left - the winner.
- It's fun to take bets at the beginning of the round on who everyone thinks will win.

DON'T SAY YES

NEED TO KNOW:

- **Number of players:** Minimum of 2 players, no maximum
- **Where to play:** Train, airplane, car

RULES:

- Choose one player to be 'on' first.
- The rest of the players ask questions and engage in conversation with the person who is 'on' with the aim of trying to make them say 'yes'.
- That person must cooperate and engage in the conversation and answer any questions asked.
- The player who successfully gets the player to say 'yes', is next to be 'on'.

TWO TRUTHS AND A LIE

NEED TO KNOW:

- **Number of players:** Minimum of 2 players, no maximum
- **Where to play:** Train, airplane, car

RULES:

- Each player takes a turn sharing three statements about themselves: two of the statements are truths, and one is a lie.
- The rest of the group collaborates to figure out which of the statements is the lie.
- For added variety, you can introduce themes for each round, such as favourite activities, unusual skills, or memorable experiences.

THE MOVIE GAME

NEED TO KNOW:

- **Number of players:** Minimum of 2 players, no maximum
- **Where to play:** Train, airplane, car

RULES:

- Choose a letter, suggested by someone in the car.
- Everyone then names movies that start with that letter, such as 'Toy Story', 'Titanic' or 'Terminator' for the letter T.
- Collectively, see how many you can name before you move on to the next letter in the alphabet and repeat the process.
- You can change the topic from movies to anything books, sports personnel, musicians, etc.

PUB CRICKET

NEED TO KNOW:

- **Number of players:** Minimum of 2 players, no maximum
- **Where to play:** car

RULES:

- This game is best played on road trips in Great Britain.
- Players spot pubs along the journey and count the number of arms and legs in each pub's name.
- Once a player has called the name of a pub, they are awarded the points only.
- For instance, 'The Red Lion' scores 4 points (4 limbs on a lion), while 'The Horse and Jockey' has 6 legs and 2 arms, reaching the maximum score of 6.
- The player with the most points at the end of the game/journey wins.

FAMOUS NAMES

NEED TO KNOW:

- **Number of players:** Minimum of 2 players, no maximum
- **Where to play:** Train, airplane

RULES:

- Start by naming a famous person (both first and last name).
- The next player must name another celebrity whose first name begins with the first letter of the previous person's last name.
- For instance, Justin Bieber leads to Billy Crystal, Billy Crystal to Catherine O'Hara, and Catherine O'Hara to Owen Wilson.
- If a player cannot think of a name, they are out, and the game continues with the remaining players, until you have a winner.

DOUBLE TROUBLE

NEED TO KNOW:

- **Number of players:** Minimum of 2 players, no maximum
- **Where to play:** Car, train, airplane

RULES:

- The game leader says a word followed by 'but not' and another word. For example, 'books, but not movies,' 'baseball, but not hockey,' or 'apples, but not oranges.'
- The leader asks the other passengers to give examples and says if they got it right or wrong.
- Secret: the first word in each pair contains a double letter, while the second does not.
- See how long it takes for the others to figure out the secret!

20 QUESTIONS

NEED TO KNOW:

- **Number of players:** Minimum of 2 players, no maximum
- **Where to play:** Car, train, airplane

RULES:

- Choose a theme for the game, such as visible objects, household items, famous actors, or singers.
- The first player thinks of a person or object and states, 'I'm thinking of a person/object'
- Players then take turns asking yes-or-no questions to identify the person or object.
- A maximum of 20 questions is allowed.
- The player who correctly guesses the person or object takes the next turn.
- If no one guesses correctly within 20 questions, the same player continues with a new person or object.

SORRY I'M LATE

NEED TO KNOW:

- **Number of players:** Minimum of 2 players, no maximum
- **Where to play:** Car, train, airplane

RULES:

- The game begins with one person saying, "Sorry I'm late..." followed by a reason that describes the plot of a movie. For example, 'Sorry I'm late because I had to save my estranged daughter, who got kidnapped while she was on a trip to Paris.'
- The others try to guess the movie based on the description. In this case, the movie is Taken.
- The person who correctly guesses the movie goes next and provides a new plot-based excuse.

HEAD COUNT

NEED TO KNOW:

- **Number of players:** Minimum of 3 players, no maximum
- **Where to play:** train, airplane, car

RULES:

- Everyone closes their eyes. If you are in the car, the driver will not be able to play (for obvious reasons!)
- The goal is to collectively count to 10 as a group.
- Any player can begin by saying 'one', followed by another player saying 'two', and so on.
- No player can say two numbers consecutively.
- If two players say a number at the same time, you must start over from zero.
- Try to reach 10 as quickly as possible. Once you succeed, challenge yourselves to reach 20!

GUESS WHOSE PLAYLIST

NEED TO KNOW:

- **Number of players:** Minimum of 4 players, no maximum
- **Where to play:** car

RULES:

- Before starting a journey, create a shared playlist - everyone has to add their 5 favourite songs to it.
- Once you're on your way, play the playlist on shuffle.
- When a song comes on, everyone has to guess who added it to the playlist.
- Use Spotify's remote group sessions to make sharing and uploading songs to the playlist easier for everyone.

ONE MINUTE CHALLENGE

NEED TO KNOW:

- **Number of players:** Minimum of 2 players, no maximum
- **Where to play:** Car, train, airplane

RULES:

- Players take turns being the speaker.
- One person keeps time for 1 minute.
- The speaker must talk about a topic of their choosing for a full minute without pausing, repeating themselves, or going off-topic. If they do, they are out.
- Rotate turns, picking a new topic each time until everyone has had a chance.
- If a minute is too difficult, you can shorten the time or see who can speak the longest on their chosen topic.

FRUIT CHARADES

NEED TO KNOW:

- **Number of players:** Minimum of 2 players, no maximum
- **Where to play:** Train, airplane

RULES:

- Players take turns miming different fruits or vegetables without speaking or using letters or words.
- Hand gestures and body movements are encouraged to help others guess.
- The player who guesses correctly gets to mime the next fruit or vegetable.
- You can mix the game up a bit by changing the mimes to animals or items you might take on a vacation.

SPIN A STORY FROM THE PAST

NEED TO KNOW:

- **Number of players:** Minimum of 2 players, no maximum
- **Where to play:** Train, airplane

RULES:

- Play a game of 'Who can lie better?' where one player shares a story from their past.
- Other players guess if the story is true or made up.
- Each guesser can ask up to two follow-up questions before making their guess.
- Correct guesses earn two points each.
- The first player to reach 10 points wins.

I'M PACKING A SUITCASE

NEED TO KNOW:

- **Number of players:** Minimum of 2 players, no maximum
- **Where to play:** Car, train, airplane

RULES:

- One player begins by saying, 'I'm packing a suitcase, and in my suitcase, I pack a...' followed by an item, such as a toothbrush.
- The next player repeats the phrase, listing the previous item and adding a new one: 'I'm packing a suitcase, and in my suitcase, I pack a toothbrush and...'
- Players take turns, each reciting the complete list of items in the correct order and adding a new one.
- If a player forgets any items, they are out of the game.
- The game continues until only one player remains, who is the winner.

ESSENTIALLY THE SAME MOVIE

NEED TO KNOW:

- **Number of players:** Minimum of 2 players, no maximum
- **Where to play:** Car, train, airplane

RULES:

- One player begins by naming a movie.
- The next player names another movie with a similar basic plot.
- For example, Pretty in Pink and Some Kind of Wonderful, or No Strings Attached and Friends with Benefits.
- Players continue taking turns naming films with essentially the same narrative.
- If a player cannot think of a fitting movie, they are out.
- The last player to successfully name a fitting film wins.

- If stuck, start with your favourite kids' movies to get the game going.

HARRY POTTER SPELLING BEE

NEED TO KNOW:

- **Number of players:** Minimum of 2 players, no maximum
- **Where to play:** Car, train, airplane

RULES:

- Play a Spelling Bee using words from a TV show, book, or movie series everyone in the car enjoys.
- Choose a theme such as Harry Potter, Star Wars, Game of Thrones, Lord of the Rings, or Grey's Anatomy medical terms.
- A player chooses a word related to the theme, and the next player must spell the word out correctly (you may need to use Google to check your answers!)
- The game continues until a player misspells a word, they are out of the round. The last person standing wins.

3

TRIVIA & RIDDLES

TRAVEL TRIVIA

Wow your fellow travel buddies with some weird and wonderful facts from around the world!

∿

Australia has a larger population of kangaroos than humans, with an estimated 50 million kangaroos hopping around the continent.

∿

Canada's national sport in the summer is lacrosse, not hockey.

∿

Russia's Trans-Siberian Railway spans nearly 9,300 km, making it the longest railway line in the world.

∿

Japan has more vending machines than people in New Zealand, offering everything from hot meals to umbrellas.

~

Brazil is the only country that has hosted the Olympics, World Cup, and has won the World Cup five times.

~

Greenland, despite its icy landscape, was named by early Viking settlers to attract more settlers.

~

India is home to a floating post office on Dal Lake in Srinagar, the only one of its kind.

~

Italy has a free public wine fountain in the town of Caldari di Ortona, offering red wine to anyone who passes by.

~

Madagascar is home to the baobab tree, which can store up to 32,000 gallons of water in its trunk.

~

Norway introduced salmon sushi to the Japanese in the 1980s, a surprising origin for such an iconic dish.

~

France's Mont-Saint-Michel becomes an island twice a day when the tide comes in, cutting it off from the mainland.

～

South Korea has a phenomenon known as "fan death," where people believe that sleeping with a fan on in a closed room can be fatal.

～

Argentina has a glacier, Perito Moreno, that is still growing, one of the few in the world.

～

China has a section of the Great Wall that's so remote, it was only rediscovered by archaeologists in 2009.

～

Switzerland consumes more chocolate per capita than any other country, averaging nearly 9 kg per person annually.

～

Kenya's Maasai Mara Reserve sees the Great Migration each year, where over 1.5 million wildebeest and hundreds of thousands of zebras and gazelles move in search of greener pastures.

～

Greece has a monastery perched on a 400-metre-high cliff, accessible only by a rope basket in the past.

~

New Zealand's Māori name is "Aotearoa," meaning "Land of the Long White Cloud."

~

Mexico City sinks about 10 cm every year because it was built on a lake bed.

~

Germany's autobahn has no speed limit on certain sections, attracting speed enthusiasts from around the world.

~

Egypt's pyramids align perfectly with the cardinal points, showcasing the ancient Egyptians' advanced understanding of astronomy.

~

Thailand has a festival called "Monkey Buffet Festival," where thousands of monkeys are fed fruits and vegetables in a huge feast.

~

Iceland's Blue Lagoon is a man-made geothermal spa and is filled with water that's rich in minerals like silica and sulphur.

≈

The United States has a state, Alaska, that is so vast it could fit Texas inside it twice, yet it has fewer people than Washington D.C.

≈

Spain's "Running of the Bulls" in Pamplona is part of the San Fermín festival, where people literally run in front of a group of bulls through the city streets.

≈

Ireland has one of the oldest pubs in the world, Sean's Bar, dating back to 900 AD.

≈

The Netherlands is so flat that the highest point in the mainland, Vaalserberg, is only 322.7 meters above sea level.

≈

Scotland has over 790 islands, but only 130 are inhabited.

≈

Finland offers "Jokamiehen Oikeus" or "Everyman's Right," allowing anyone to roam freely in nature, camp, and forage regardless of land ownership.

~

Antarctica is the only continent without a native insect population, making it the most sterile place on Earth.

~

The world's longest commercial flight is from New York to Singapore, covering a distance of approximately 15,349 km in nearly 19 hours.

~

Monaco is the second smallest country in the world, smaller than New York's Central Park, yet it boasts the highest number of millionaires per capita.

~

The Panama Canal's expansion project, completed in 2016, allows for the passage of ships that are 2.5 times the size of the ones previously accommodated.

~

Venice's Grand Canal is crossed by only four bridges, despite being one of the busiest waterways in the world.

~

Dubai's Burj Khalifa not only holds the title of the tallest building in the world but also has the highest observation deck, at a dizzying 555 meters.

~

Hawaii is the only U.S. state that grows coffee, thanks to its unique climate and volcanic soil.

~

France has more than 1,000 different types of cheese, from Brie to Roquefort, making it a paradise for cheese lovers.

~

Portugal's Azores islands are home to some of the world's most stunning natural landscapes, including volcanic crater lakes and waterfalls.

~

Brazil's Christ the Redeemer statue was struck by lightning in 2014, which damaged its right thumb.

~

Mount Everest is littered with more than 50 tons of trash, left behind by climbers over the years.

~

Australia's pink Lake Hillier gets its unusual color from a type of algae that thrives in its salty environment.

~

Japan's bullet trains, known as Shinkansen, are so fast and smooth that a passenger could balance a coin on its edge during the journey.

～

Scotland's Highland Games feature unique events like caber tossing, where participants flip a large log end-over-end.

～

Sweden's Icehotel, built each year from ice harvested from the nearby Torne River, melts away in the spring, only to be rebuilt anew.

～

Italy's Leaning Tower of Pisa leans because of unstable foundation soil, but it has been stabilized to prevent further tilting.

～

Mexico's Island of the Dolls, located in the canals of Xochimilco, is covered with creepy dolls hanging from trees and buildings.

～

South Africa's Table Mountain has more plant species within its 22,000 hectares than the entire British Isles.

～

Iceland's Strokkur Geyser erupts every 6-10 minutes, shooting water up to 40 meters high.

～

Mongolia's Gobi Desert is home to a rare species of camel that can drink salty water without getting sick.

～

Norway's Svalbard Global Seed Vault, often called the "Doomsday Vault," preserves seeds from around the world in case of global catastrophe.

～

Argentina's Valdés Peninsula is one of the few places in the world where orcas intentionally beach themselves to hunt seals.

～

Nepal's Kathmandu Valley contains seven UNESCO World Heritage Sites, each within a 20 km radius.

～

Vietnam's Hang Son Doong, the world's largest cave, has its own weather system, with clouds forming inside the cave.

～

Switzerland's Matterhorn is one of the most photographed

mountains in the world, often mistaken as a pyramid due to its shape.

~

Jordan's ancient city of Petra was unknown to the Western world until 1812, when it was rediscovered by a Swiss explorer.

~

Denmark's Copenhagen is home to the world's oldest amusement park, Bakken, which dates back to 1583.

~

Bolivia's Salar de Uyuni, the world's largest salt flat, becomes a giant mirror during the rainy season, reflecting the sky perfectly.

~

Australia's Great Barrier Reef is so large it can be seen from space and is home to more than 1,500 species of fish.

~

The United States' Yellowstone National Park was the first national park in the world, established in 1872.

~

France's Eiffel Tower was originally intended to be

dismantled after 20 years but was saved because it became useful as a giant radio antenna.

RIDDLES

1. I speak without a mouth and hear without ears. I have no body, but I come alive with wind. What am I?

~

2. You measure my life in hours and I serve you by expiring. I'm quick when I'm thin and slow when I'm fat. The wind is my enemy. What am I?

~

3. I have cities, but no houses. I have mountains, but no trees. I have water, but no fish. What am I?

~

4. What can run but never walks, has a mouth but never talks, has a head but never weeps, has a bed but never sleeps?

～

5. The more you take, the more you leave behind. What am I?

～

6. What has keys but can't open locks?

～

7. What is seen in the middle of March and April that can't be seen at the beginning or end of either month?

～

8. I come from a mine and get surrounded by wood always. Everyone uses me. What am I?

～

9. What can fill a room but takes up no space?

～

10. What has one eye but can't see?

~

11. I have branches, but no fruit, trunk, or leaves. What am I?

~

12. The person who makes it, sells it. The person who buys it never uses it. The person who uses it never knows they're using it. What is it?

~

13. What has to be broken before you can use it?

~

14. I'm light as a feather, yet the strongest man can't hold me for much more than a minute. What am I?

~

15. What has many keys but can't open a single lock?

~

16. I'm not alive, but I can grow; I don't have lungs, but I need air; I don't have a mouth, and I can drown. What am I?

∼

17. I shave every day, but my beard stays the same. What am I?

∼

18. What has lots of eyes, but can't see?

∼

19. I have no life, but I can die. What am I?

∼

20. What begins with T, ends with T, and has T in it?

∼

21. What gets bigger when more is taken away?

∼

22. I'm tall when I'm young, and I'm short when I'm old. What am I?

≈

23. What can travel around the world while staying in a corner?

≈

24. What has an eye but cannot see?

≈

25. What is always in front of you but can't be seen?

≈

26. What gets wetter the more it dries?

≈

27. What comes once in a minute, twice in a moment, but never in a thousand years?

≈

28. What has a head, a tail, is brown, and has no legs?

≈

29. I can be cracked, made, told, and played. What am I?

~

30. What is so fragile that saying its name breaks it?

4

CONVERSATION STARTERS

WOULD YOU RATHER...

Would you rather go on a road trip across your country or fly to a foreign country?

~

Would you rather travel to a beach destination or a mountain retreat?

~

Would you rather go on a vacation to a bustling city or quiet countryside?

~

Would you rather take a scenic train ride or a luxury cruise?

~

Would you rather visit famous tourist spots or discover hidden gems?

~

Would you rather travel with a group of friends or solo?

~

Would you rather take a red-eye flight and arrive in the morning or fly during the day and arrive in the evening?

~

Would you rather go camping in the wilderness or stay in a 5-star hotel?

~

Would you rather travel to a place with extreme heat or extreme cold?

~

Would you rather spend a week at an all-inclusive resort or a weekend in a city of your choice?

~

Would you rather drive a convertible along a coastal highway or an SUV through the mountains?

~

Would you rather go on a safari in Africa or explore the Great Barrier Reef in Australia?

~

Would you rather visit a famous theme park or a renowned museum?

~

Would you rather have a vacation planned to every detail or be spontaneous and go with the flow?

~

Would you rather travel to a place where you don't speak the language or a place where you don't know anyone?

~

Would you rather fly in first class or stay in a luxury hotel?

~

Would you rather go on a culinary tour or an adventure tour?

~

Would you rather take a sabbatical to explore Asia or Africa?

~

Would you rather travel by car for a long road trip or take multiple short flights?

~

Would you rather visit all the countries in Europe or explore all the states in the USA?

~

Would you rather have a relaxing vacation by the pool or an active vacation with lots of excursions?

~

Would you rather travel to a famous festival or a quiet retreat?

~

Would you rather go on a cruise to Alaska or a Caribbean cruise?

~

Would you rather visit a new city every day or stay in one city for your entire trip?

~

Would you rather travel to a place known for its food or its shopping?

~

Would you rather go on a road trip with family or friends?

~

Would you rather the airline lost your luggage or you fell ill on the first day of your holiday?

~

Would you rather have a vacation with a colleague who you find really boring or with a family member who annoys you?

~

Would you rather get up early to see the sunrise or stay up late to watch the sunset?

～

Would you rather make swimming in the sea the first thing you do on your vacation or drink a cocktail?

～

Would you rather visit a famous film location or a renowned music festival?

～

Would you rather experience a hot air balloon ride or a helicopter tour?

～

Would you rather spend a night in a haunted hotel or a luxury treehouse?

～

Would you rather try street food in Asia or dine at a Michelin-star restaurant in Europe?

～

Would you rather go scuba diving in the Maldives or hiking in the Swiss Alps?

~

Would you rather attend a major sporting event or a prestigious cultural event?

~

Would you rather have a vacation without any phone signal or without being able to take photos?

~

Would you rather take a historic walking tour or a modern art tour?

~

Would you rather visit a tropical island or a remote desert?

~

Would you rather experience the nightlife in a famous city or the tranquility of a rural village?

~

Would you rather travel during peak tourist season or off-season, even if it means some places will be shut?

~

Would you rather abseil off a famous landmark or sleep overnight in a museum?

~

Would you rather go on a guided tour or explore independently?

~

Would you rather travel with a strict budget or splurge on luxury experiences?

~

Would you rather spend time in a bustling market or a quiet library?

~

Would you rather stay in a historical castle or a modern skyscraper hotel?

~

Would you rather have an adventure holiday full of adrenaline sports or a wellness retreat focused on relaxation?

∼

Would you rather visit a wine region for tastings or a chocolate factory for samplings?

∼

Would you rather travel to a place famous for its sunsets or its night sky?

∼

Would you rather go whale watching in the ocean or stargazing in a desert?

∼

Would you rather visit the pyramids or see the Northern Lights?

∼

Would you rather hike through a dense forest or walk along a scenic coastline?

∼

Would you rather do a walking vacation or a cycling vacation?

～

Would you rather be restricted on a city break to only eating one meal during your whole vacation or only being able to explore a single street?

～

Would you rather take a do a camel trek in the Sahara desert or or husky dog sledge tour in Norway?

～

Would you rather climb do a long multi-day train ride or a cruise?

～

Would you rather attend a live theatre performance or a concert?

～

Would you rather stay in an eco-friendly lodge or a high-tech hotel?

～

Would you rather spend a weekend visiting New York City or London

∾

Would you rather spend a year travelling on a tight budget or a month travelling in luxury?

TELL ME ABOUT...

Tell me about your favourite vacation that you've ever taken.

~

Tell me about a time you tried something new and loved it.

~

Tell me about a place you've always dreamed of visiting.

~

Tell me about a memorable road trip you've been on.

~

Tell me about your childhood home.

~

Tell me about a hobby or activity you're passionate about.

~

Tell me about a goal you're currently working towards.

~

Tell me about the best meal you've ever had while travelling.

~

Tell me about a book or movie that changed your perspective on life.

~

Tell me about a person who has had a significant impact on your life.

~

Tell me about a challenge you've overcome.

~

Tell me about an unusual tradition your family has.

~

Tell me about a time you got lost but ended up discovering something amazing.

~

Tell me about your dream job.

~

Tell me about a time you helped someone in need.

~

Tell me about a skill you've always wanted to learn.

~

Tell me about the most interesting person you've ever met.

~

Tell me about a favourite childhood memory.

~

Tell me about a time you felt really proud of yourself.

~

Tell me about a pet you've had or would like to have.

~

Tell me about a funny or embarrassing moment from your past.

~

Tell me about your ideal weekend.

~

Tell me about a project or accomplishment you're particularly proud of.

~

Tell me about a time you stepped out of your comfort zone.

~

Tell me about a place you feel most at peace.

∼

Tell me about your favourite way to relax.

∼

Tell me about a concert or event you'll never forget.

∼

Tell me about a dream you had that felt very real.

∼

Tell me about a time you made a difficult decision.

∼

Tell me about a favourite family recipe or meal.

∼

Tell me about a book that had a profound impact on your life and why.

∼

Tell me about a life lesson you learned the hard way.

~

Tell me about a time you faced a significant challenge and how you overcame it.

~

Tell me about a mentor or role model who influenced you and how they impacted your life.

~

Tell me about a dream or aspiration you had as a child and whether it has changed over time.

~

Tell me about a cultural experience or event that broadened your perspective.

~

Tell me about a turning point in your life and how it shaped who you are today.

~

Tell me about a career decision you made that significantly altered your path.

～

Tell me about a time you had to make a difficult choice and the factors that influenced your decision.

～

Tell me about a place that holds a special meaning for you and why.

～

Tell me about a personal project or hobby that you're passionate about and how you got started.

～

Tell me about a time you experienced a random act of kindness and how it affected you.

～

Tell me about a goal you set for yourself and the steps you took to achieve it.

～

Tell me about a historical event that you wish you could have witnessed and why.

~

Tell me about a time you pushed yourself out of your comfort zone and the outcome.

~

Tell me about a personal value or principle that you hold dear and how it guides your decisions.

~

Tell me about a memorable conversation that changed your outlook on life.

~

Tell me about a travel experience that was transformative and why.

~

Tell me about a habit or routine that significantly improves your day-to-day life.

~

Tell me about a creative endeavour you embarked on and what you learned from the process.

∼

Tell me about a personal value or principle that you hold dear and how it guides your decisions.

∼

Tell me about a moment when you've felt really scared.

∼

Tell me about a special travel experience that sticks in your mind.

∼

Tell me about something you do that is quirky that very few people know about.

∼

Tell me about something you've done that you don't feel proud of and what you'd do differently now.

∼

Tell me about a time when a stranger became a friend.

~

Tell me about a piece of advice that has stuck with you over the years.

~

Tell me about what your go-to activity or habit is when you feel stressed and need to unwind.

~

Tell me about a time you felt truly connected to nature.

~

Tell me about a personal achievement that made you realise your potential.

WHAT WOULD YOU DO IF....

What would you do if you won the lottery tomorrow?

~

What would you do if you could travel back in time for a day?

~

What would you do if you were invisible for 24 hours?

~

What would you do if you could have dinner with any historical figure?

~

What would you do if you could live anywhere in the world?

~

What would you do if you had the ability to read minds?

~

What would you do if you found a suitcase full of money?

~

What would you do if you could switch lives with someone for a week?

~

What would you do if you could speak any language fluently?

~

What would you do if you could only eat one food for the rest of your life?

~

What would you do if you discovered you could fly?

～

What would you do if you were the President or Prime Minister for a day?

～

What would you do if you could meet your favourite celebrity?

～

What would you do if you were stranded on a deserted island?

～

What would you do if you had to start your life over in a different country?

～

What would you do if you could see the future?

～

What would you do if you could instantly learn a new skill?

～

What would you do if you could swap jobs with anyone?

～

What would you do if you were given a chance to live in space for a year?

～

What would you do if you could only listen to one song for the rest of your life?

～

What would you do if you had to live without the internet for a month?

～

What would you do if you could solve one major world problem?

～

What would you do if you could relive any moment in your life?

～

What would you do if you had to start a new course or study a new subject?

～

What would you do if you found out you had a long-lost sibling?

～

What would you do if you could spend a day in the life of your favourite fictional character?

～

What would you do if you could teleport anywhere in the world?

～

What would you do if you could time travel to the future?

～

What would you do if you had to give up one of your senses for a year?

~

What would you do if you could make one wish come true?

~

What would you do if you found out you only had a year to leave?

5

QUIZES

GUESS THE MOVIE

Can you guess all these films correctly with just 6 or less word plot lines?

Find the answers at the end of the book!

∼

1. Mafia family, power struggle, betrayal.

∼

2. Man in box, desert rescue.

∼

3. Man freed, gladiator, revenge mission.

∼

4. Boat sinks, love story, tragedy.

~

5. Vietnam war, mission, insane colonel.

~

6. Mysterious island, dinosaurs, danger, escape.

~

7. Clown crime spree, vigilante hero battles.

~

8. Boxing underdog, rises, championship fight.

~

9. Detective investigates, hidden clues, wife's disappearance.

~

10. Heist gone wrong, suspects, warehouse standoff.

~

11. Southern lawyer, racial injustice, court battle.

～

12. Space opera, rebel fight, dark lord.

～

13. Brothers reunite, autistic savant, road trip.

～

14. Virtual reality, hacker, chosen one.

～

15. Time-traveling car, past changes, future fixes.

～

16. Desperate cops, intense chase, tense showdown.

～

18. King returns, battle, Middle-earth saved.

～

19. Mind-bending dreams, corporate espionage, architect.

~

20. Fearless archaeologist, quest for holy relic.

~

21. Alien invasion, White House destroyed, resistance.

~

22. Disfigured musical genius, opera house.

~

23. Southern women, friendship, life's challenges.

~

24. Author's secret, reclusive writer, hidden identity.

~

25. Ruthless stockbroker, financial crime spree.

~

26. Dance competition, underdog couple, triumph.

～

27. Ruthless killer, silent stalker, babysitter.

～

28. Love and madness, circus performers.

～

29. Detective doggedly pursues, seedy underworld exposed.

～

30. College students, wild party, unexpected consequences.

～

31. Conman duo, big score, betrayal.

～

32. Elderly romance, Alzheimer's, enduring love.

～

33. Magical nanny, children's adventure, life lessons.

~

34. Prodigal son, African throne, epic journey.

~

35. Hitman mentor, assassin protege, lethal partnership.

~

36. Undercover cop, Boston crime saga, mole.

~

37. Southern farmer, baseball, ghost players.

~

38. Hidden family secret, forbidden love, tragedy.

~

39. Heist team, mastermind, intricate plan.

~

40. Astronaut stranded, survives Mars, rescue mission.

~

41. Mysterious briefcase, boxer, gangster, intertwining stories.

~

42. Mob boss, two sons, different paths.

~

43. Superhero team assembles, fights alien invasion.

~

44. Terminal illness, bucket list, adventures begin.

~

45. Unlikely duo, solve crimes, British detectives.

~

46. Giant ape, skyscraper, epic battle.

~

47. Post-apocalyptic world, mother, daughter survive.

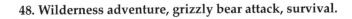

48. Wilderness adventure, grizzly bear attack, survival.

49. Surfer girl, shark attack, comeback story.

50. Love, time travel, second chances, romance.

ROAD TRIP QUIZ

Test you and your passengers out with this Road Trip Trivia quiz.

Find the answers at the end of the book!

1. What is the capital of Australia?

2. Which country is known as the Land of the Rising Sun?

3. In which US state is the Grand Canyon located?

4. What is the longest river in the world?

5. Which city is famous for its canals and gondolas?

6. Which is the smallest country in the world by area?

7. In which country can you visit Machu Picchu?

8. What language is spoken in Brazil?

9. Which is the most populous country in Africa?

10. Which city is home to the Colosseum?

11. What is the capital city of Canada?

12. Which is the largest hot desert in the world?

13. Which country is both a continent and a country?

14. What is the currency of Japan?

15. Which city is known as the City of Light?

16. In which country can you find the Leaning Tower of Pisa?

17. What is the highest mountain in Africa?

18. Which city is often referred to as the Eternal City?

19. What river flows through Paris?

20. In which country is the city of Dubai located?

21. What is the capital city of Egypt?

22. Which island nation is located off the southeastern coast of Africa?

23. Which country is known for its beautiful coastline along the Adriatic Sea and the historic city of Dubrovnik?

24. What is the capital city of Argentina?

25. Which US city is famous for its country music scene?

26. Which country is famous for its Carnival festival in Rio de Janeiro?

27. Which Scandinavian country is known for its fjords and Vikings?

28. What is the capital city of Thailand?

29. Which country is known for its bullet trains and cherry blossoms?

30. Which Caribbean island is known for its reggae music?

31. What is the capital city of South Korea?

32. Which country is famous for its chocolate, watches, and banking?

33. Which desert is located in northern China and southern Mongolia?

34. In which Middle Eastern country can you find the ancient city of Petra?

35. What is the official language of Egypt?

36. Which US state is home to Walt Disney World?

37. Which famous public square is located in Moscow?

38. In which country can you find the Matterhorn?

39. What is the capital city of Malaysia?

40. Which country is famous for its ancient mythology and the Parthenon?

41. In which country can you visit the Pyramids of Giza?

42. What is the capital city of Portugal?

43. Which US state is home to Hollywood?

44. What is the official language of Spain?

45. Which country is famous for its tango dance and beef production?

46. Which country is known for its art, culture, and cuisine, and is home to the cities of Rome and Venice?

47. What is the capital city of New Zealand?

48. In which country can you find the Dead Sea?

49. Which city is home to the famous Sydney Opera House?

50. What is the capital city of Russia?

6

THANK YOU!

Thank you for purchasing a copy of my book!

As a small independent author, I rely heavily on reviews so that others might also find and purchase my books. So I'd be hugely grateful if you could spare a few moments to leave me a review...

....Thank you!

It always brings me a lot of joy to hear from readers. Tag me in any photos of your reading the book, or trying out any of the games. Or just drop me a message to say 'hello'....

Instagram: @Bex_Band

Facebook: /BexBand

YouTube: @BandFamilyAdventures

Newsletter: www.theordinaryadventurer.com/sign-up/

ANY WOMEN READING?

Don't forget to check out Love Her Wild - the women's adventure community I founded.

Now with tens of thousands of members, Love Her Wild is responsible for getting thousands of women on adventures each year.

It's free to become a member and there's loads for you to get involved with...

...women-only adventures and expeditions

...free get-togethers and meet-ups

...grants to support more women to get outdoors

... an online hub full of ideas and inspiration

At Love Her Wild, we pride ourselves on being the friendliest and most inclusive outdoor community.

Check out our website for more ways we can help bring adventure to your life: www.LoveHerWild.com

RIDDLE: ANSWERS

1. *An echo*
2. *A candle*
3. *A map*
4. *A river*
5. *Footsteps*
6. *A piano*
7. *The letter 'R'*
8. *Pencil lead*
9. *Light*
10. *A needle*
11. *A bank*
12. *A coffin*
13. *An egg*
14. *Your breath*
15. *A piano*
16. *Fire*
17. *A barber*
18. *A potato*
19. *A battery*
20. *A teapot*
21. *A hole*

22. *A candle*
23. *A stamp*
24. *A needle*
25. *The future*
26. *A towel*
27. *The letter 'M'*
28. *A penny*
29. *A joke*
30. *Silence*

GUESS THE MOVIE: ANSWERS

1. *The Godfather*
2. *Buried*
3. *Gladiator*
4. *Titanic*
5. *Apocalypse Now*
6. *Jurassic Park*
7. *The Dark Knight*
8. *Rocky*
9. *Gone Girl*
10. *Reservoir Dogs*
11. *To Kill a Mockingbird*
12. *Star Wars*
13. *Rain Man*
14. *The Matrix*
15. *Back to the Future*
16. *Heat*
17. *The Shining*
18. *The Lord of the Rings: The Return of the King*
19. *Inception*
20. *Indiana Jones and the Last Crusade*
21. *Independence Day*

ROAD TRIP TRIVIA: ANSWERS

1. *Canberra*
2. *Japan*
3. *Arizona*
4. *Nile River*
5. *Venice*
6. *Vatican City*
7. *Peru*
8. *Portuguese*
9. *Nigeria*
10. *Rome*
11. *Ottawa*
12. *Sahara Desert*
13. *Australia*
14. *Yen*
15. *Paris*
16. *Italy*
17. *Mount Kilimanjaro*
18. *Rome*
19. *Seine*
20. *United Arab Emirates*
21. *Cairo*

22. *Madagascar*
23. *Croatia*
24. *Buenos Aires*
25. *Nashville*
26. *Brazil*
27. *Norway*
28. *Bangkok*
29. *Japan*
30. *Jamaica*
31. *Seoul*
32. *Switzerland*
33. *Gobi Desert*
34. *Jordan*
35. *Arabic*
36. *Florida*
37. *Red Square*
38. *Switzerland*
39. *Kuala Lumpur*
40. *Greece*
41. *Egypt*
42. *Lisbon*
43. *California*
44. *Spanish*
45. *Argentina*
46. *Italy*
47. *Wellington*
48. *Jordan*
49. *Sydney*
50. *Moscow*

Made in the USA
Monee, IL
21 July 2025

21625095R00066